SCHOLASTIC

Perfect Poems

With Strategies for Building Fluency

Grades 5–6

NEW YORK • TORONTO • LONDON • AUCKLAND • SYDNEY
MEXICO CITY • NEW DELHI • HONG KONG • BUENOS AIRES

Teaching Resources

ACKNOWLEDGMENTS

Every effort has been made to contact copyright holders for permission to reproduce borrowed material. The publisher regrets any oversights that may have occurred and will be pleased to rectify them in subsequent reprints of the work.

The material on pages 4–13 has been adapted from BUILDING FLUENCY: LESSONS AND STRATEGIES FOR READING SUCCESS by Wiley Blevins (Scholastic, 2001). Adapted and reprinted by permission of the publisher.

"Cloud Brothers" from SILENT WINDS POEMS OF A HOPI by Ramson Lomatewama, by permission of the author.

"How Many Legs?" and "Mom's Allergic" copyright © 1999 by Mary Sullivan. Used by permission of the author.

"Languages My Neighbors Speak" copyright © 2000 by Linda Bendor. Reprinted by permission of the author.

"Seven Days of Supper" copyright © 1997 by Dorothy Jean Sklar. Reprinted by permission of the author.

"Earth, What Will You Give Me?" by Beverly McLoughland. First appeared in *Humpty Dumpty* Magazine, Nov. 1997. All rights reserved by Benjamin Franklin Literary & Medical Society.

"Wondering" copyright © 1992 by Bobbi Katz. Used by permission of the author.

"Zoons" by Florence E. Sullivan. Copyright © 1990 by Scholastic Inc. Used by permission of the publisher.

"Foul Shot" by Edwin A. Hoey is reprinted from *Read* Magazine. Copyright © 1962 by Xerox Education Publications. Reprinted by permission of *Read* Magazine, published by Weekly Reader Corporation.

"Leap Year Lament" copyright © 1999 by Jacqueline Sweeney. Used by permission of Marian Reiner for the author.

"Time for Bed" by Amanda Miller. Copyright © by Scholastic Inc. Used by permission of the publisher.

"See How They Run!" by Grace Mayr. Copyright © 1990 by Scholastic Inc. Used by permission of the publisher.

"Spelling Test" copyright © 2000 by Linda Ross. Used by permission of the author.

"The Red Ball" copyright © 1997 by Liza Charlesworth. Reprinted by permission of the author.

"City I Love" by Lee Bennett Hopkins. From HOME TO ME by Lee Bennett Hopkins. Copyright © 2002 by Lee Bennett Hopkins. Reprinted by permission of Orchard Books, an imprint of Scholastic Inc.

"Some Poems" copyright © 1992 by Beverly McLoughland. Used by permission of the author who controls all rights.

"Words" by Glenda Greve. Copyright © 1990 by Scholastic Inc. Used by permission of the publisher.

"A Magic Chant" copyright © 1994 by Bobbi Katz. Used by permission of the author.

"Animal Groups" from 101 SCIENCE POEMS AND SONGS FOR YOUNG LEARNERS by Meish Goldish. Copyright © 1996 by Meish Goldish. Reprinted by permission of the author.

"A Secret in My Pocket" by Karen Baicker. Copyright © by Scholastic Inc. Used by permission of the publisher.

"Paul Bunyan" by Meish Goldish from ONCE UPON A TIME IN RHYME: 28 FOLK AND FAIRY TALE POEMS AND SONGS. Copyright © 1995 by Scholastic Inc. Used by permission of the publisher.

"He Had a Dream" by Meish Goldish from THEMATIC POEMS, SONGS, AND FINGERPLAYS. Copyright © 1993 by Scholastic Inc. Used by permission of the publisher.

"American Heritage" by Elsie Walush. Copyright © 1990 by Scholastic Inc. Used by permission of the publisher.

"I Don't Want To" from IT'S RAINING PIGS AND NOODLES by Jack Prelutsky. Copyright © 2000 by Jack Prelutsky. Used by permission of HarperCollins Publishers.

"Granny and the Broomstick" by Andrew Matthews. Copyright © by Andrew Matthews. Reprinted by permission of The Peters Fraser and Dunlop Group Limited on behalf of Andrew Matthews.

"My Brother Bert" from MEET MY FOLKS by Ted Hughes. Copyright © 1961 by Ted Hughes. Reprinted with the permission of Simon & Schuster Children's Publishing Division and Faber and Faber Ltd.

From "Adventures of Isabel" by Ogden Nash. From THE BAD PARENT'S GARDEN OF VERSE by Ogden Nash. Copyright © 1968 by Ogden Nash. Reprinted by permission of Curtis Brown Ltd.

"Sick" from WHERE THE SIDEWALK ENDS by Shel Silverstein. Copyright © 1974 by Evil Eye Music, Inc. Used by permission of HarperCollins Publishers.

"Fudge" from RAINY, RAINY SATURDAY by Jack Prelutsky. Copyright © 1980 by Jack Prelutsky. Used by permission of HarperCollins Publishers.

Cover design by Maria Lilja
Interior illustrations by Delana Bettoli, Kate Flanagen, Brian Floca,
Mike Gordon, Mark A. Hicks, and Mike Moran
Interior design by Holly Grundon

ISBN: 0-439-56021-7

Contents

What Is Reading Fluency?

Fluency: A Definition

Listening to children read—whether it's a piece of their own writing or an excerpt from a favorite trade book—can tell us a lot about their reading progress. An oral reading that is smooth, accurate, and that uses the correct intonation and phrasing reflects a reader who understands the text and has mastered basic decoding skills. An oral reading that is slow, labored, and lacking in expression is characteristic of a child who lacks reading proficiency or is reading a text beyond his or her reading level. Therefore, a child's reading fluency is one important measure of a child's reading progress.

According to *A Dictionary of Reading and Related Terms* (Harris and Hodges, 1981), fluency is "the ability to read smoothly, easily, and readily with freedom from word-recognition problems." Fluency is necessary for good comprehension and enjoyable reading (Nathan and Stanovich, 1991). A lack of fluency is characterized by a slow, halting pace; frequent mistakes; poor phrasing; and inadequate intonation (Samuels, 1979)—all the result of weak word-recognition skills.

Fluent reading is a major goal of reading instruction because decoding print accurately and effortlessly enables students to read for meaning. According to Chall's Stages of Reading Development, fluency begins around grades 2 to 3 for many students. During this fluency stage, the reader becomes "unglued" from the print; that is, students can recognize many words quickly and accurately by sight and are skilled at sounding out those they don't recognize. For some students, however, fluency requires additional instruction and guided practice in foundational skills throughout the elementary years. Basically, a fluent reader can:

1. **read at a rapid rate (pace—the speed at which oral or silent reading occurs).**

2. **automatically recognize words (smoothness/accuracy—efficient decoding skills).**

3. **phrase correctly (prosody—the ability to read a text orally using appropriate pitch, stress, and phrasing).**

Nonfluent readers read slowly and spend so much time trying to identify unfamiliar words that they have trouble comprehending what they're reading.

Automaticity theory, developed by LaBerge and Samuels (1974) helps explain how reading fluency develops. Automaticity refers to knowing how to do something so well you don't have to think about it. As tasks become easier, they require less attention and practice. Think of a child learning to play basketball. As initial attention is focused on how to dribble the ball, it's difficult for the child to think about guarding the ball from opponents, shooting a basket, or even running quickly down the court. However, over time, lots of practice makes dribbling almost second nature. The player is ready to concentrate on higher-level aspects of the game.

For reading, automaticity refers to the ability to accurately and quickly recognize many words as whole units. The advantage of recognizing a word as a whole unit is that words have meaning, and less memory is required for a meaningful word than for a meaningless letter. The average child needs between 4 and 14 exposures to a new word to recognize it automatically. However, children with reading difficulties need 40 or more exposures to a new word. Therefore, it's critical that students get a great deal of practice reading texts at their independent reading level to develop automaticity (Beck & Juel, 1995; Samuels, Schermer & Reinking, 1992).

To commit words to memory, children need to decode many words sound by sound, and then progress to recognizing the larger word chunks. Then, instead of focusing on sounding out words sound by sound, the reader can read whole words, thereby focusing attention on decoding and comprehension simultaneously. In fact, the hallmark of fluent reading is the ability to decode and comprehend at the same time.

Although research has shown that fluency is a critical factor in reading development, many teachers and publishers have failed to recognize its importance to overall reading proficiency. Few teachers teach fluency directly, and elementary reading textbooks give fluency instruction short shrift. Consequently, Allington (1983) has called fluency the "neglected goal" of reading instruction.

There are many reasons why children fail to read fluently. They include the following (Allington, 1983; Blevins, 2002):

Lack of foundational skills

Some children have not mastered basic decoding skills or sight word recognition of the most frequent words in text. Therefore, when they are confronted with more complex text containing longer sentences and more multisyllabic words, their reading breaks down.

Lack of practice time

Good readers generally spend more time reading during instructional time and therefore become better readers. Good readers also engage in more silent reading. This additional practice stimulates their reading growth. Poor readers spend less time actually reading.

Frustration

Good readers are exposed to more text at their independent reading level, whereas poor readers frequently encounter text at their frustration level. Consequently poor readers tend to give up because they make so many errors.

Lack of exposure

Some children have never been exposed to fluent reading models. These children come from homes in which there are few books and little or no reading.

Missing the "why" of reading

Good readers tend to view reading as making meaning from text, whereas poor readers tend to view reading as trying to read words accurately.

The good-reader syndrome

In school, good readers are more likely to get positive feedback and more likely to be encouraged to read with expression and make meaning from text. Poor readers receive less positive feedback and the focus of their instruction is often solely on figuring out words or attending to word parts.

How to Develop Fluency

Although few reading-textbook teacher manuals contain instruction on building fluency, there are in fact many things you can do to develop your students' fluency. Rasinski (1989) has identified six key ways to build fluency.

1. Model fluent reading

Students need many opportunities to hear texts read. This can include daily teacher read alouds, books on tape, poems, and texts read by peers during sharing time. It's particularly critical for poorer readers who've been placed in a low reading group to hear text read correctly because they are likely to repeatedly hear the efforts of other poor readers in their group. They need proficient, fluent models; that is, they need to have a model voice in their heads to refer to as they monitor their own reading. While you read aloud to students, periodically highlight aspects of fluent reading. For example, point out how you read dialogue the way you think the character might have said it or how you speed up your reading when the text becomes more intense and exciting. Talk about fluency—how to achieve it, and why it's important. Constantly remind students that with practice they can become fluent readers. An important benefit of daily read alouds is that they expose students to a wider range of vocabulary.

2. Provide direct instruction and feedback

Direct instruction and feedback in fluency includes, but isn't limited to, independent reading practice, fluent reading modeling, and monitoring students' reading rates. Here are some ways to include lots of this needed instruction in your classroom.

* Explicitly teach students sound-spelling correspondences they struggle with, high-utility decoding and syllabication strategies, and a large core of sight words.

* Occasionally time students' reading. Have students create charts to monitor their own progress. Encourage them to set new reading-rate goals.

* Find alternatives to round-robin reading. Round-robin reading is one of the most harmful techniques for developing fluency. During round-robin reading, students read aloud only a small portion of the text. Although they are supposed to be following along with the

other readers, often they don't. It is absolutely essential that students read a lot every day. When they're reading a new story or poem, it is important that they read the entire text—often more than once. One way to avoid round-robin reading is to have students read the text silently a few pages at a time and then ask them questions or have them comment on strategies they used. Other appropriate techniques include partner reading, reading softly to themselves while you circulate and "listen in," and popcorn reading, in which students are called on frequently and randomly (often in the middle of a paragraph or stanza) to read aloud. If you use any technique in which students have not read the entire text during their reading group, be sure that they read it in its entirety before or after the reading group.

❀ Teach appropriate phrasing and intonation. Guided oral reading practice and the study of punctuation and grammar can help. For teaching phrasing, see phrase-cued text practice on page 11. For teaching intonation and punctuation, use some or all of the following. Have students:

◆ recite the alphabet as a conversation.
ABCD? EFG! HI? JKL. MN? OPQ. RST! UVWX. YZ!

◆ recite the same sentence using different punctuation.
Cows moo. Cows moo? Cows moo!

◆ practice placing the stress on different words in the same sentence.
I am happy. I <u>am</u> happy. I am <u>happy</u>.

◆ practice reading sentences as if talking to a friend.

Studying grammar fosters fluency because grammar alerts the reader to natural phrases in a sentence. For example, being able to identify the subject and the predicate of a sentence is one step in understanding phrase boundaries in text. Also, understanding the role of prepositions and conjunctions adds additional clues to phrase boundaries. Try providing students with short passages color-coded according to subject and predicate to assist them in practice reading.

❀ Conduct 2-minute drills to underline or locate a target word, syllable, or spelling pattern in an array or short passage (Moats, 1998). This will help students rapidly recognize spelling patterns that are common to many words. And it's a lot of fun.

3. Provide reader support (choral reading and reading-while-listening)

Readers need to practice reading both orally and silently. Research has shown that oral reading is very important for the developing reader, especially younger children. It appears that young children need to hear themselves read, and they benefit from adult feedback. As well as improving reading, this feedback shows students how highly we adults value the skill of reading. There are several ways to support students' oral reading without evoking the fear and humiliation struggling readers often feel when called on to read aloud. Here are the most popular techniques (always use text at the student's instructional level that models natural language patterns).

- Reading simultaneously with a partner or small group. With this technique, students can "float" in and out as appropriate without feeling singled out. For best results, have students practice reading the selection independently before reading it with the partner or group.

- Echo reading. As you read a phrase or sentence in the text, the student repeats it. This continues throughout the text. You can also use a tape recording of the text with pauses for the child to echo the reading.

- Choral reading. Reading together as a group is great for poetry and selections with a distinct pattern. Students are challenged to read at the same pace and with the same phrasing and intonation as the rest of the group.

- Paired repeated readings (Koskinen and Blum, 1986). A student reads a short text three times to a partner and gets feedback. Then the partners switch roles. To avoid frustration, it works best to pair above-level readers with on-level readers and on-level readers with below-level readers.

- Books and poems on tape. Select and place appropriate books and poems on tape in a classroom Listening Center. Have students follow along as the text is read, reading with the narrator where possible.

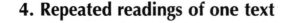

4. Repeated readings of one text

Repeated reading, a popular technique developed by Samuels (1979), has long been recognized as an excellent way to help students achieve fluency. It has been shown to increase reading rate and accuracy and to transfer to new texts. As a child reads a passage at his or her instructional level, the teacher times the reading. The teacher then gives feedback on word-recognition errors and the number of words per minute the child read accurately, and records this data on a graph. (To use poetry for repeated readings in grades 5–6, the poem should contain about 150 words.) The child then practices reading the same selection independently or with a partner. The process is repeated and the child's progress plotted on the graph until the child masters the text. This charting is effective because (1) students become focused on their own mastery of the task and competing with their own past performance, and (2) students have concrete evidence that they are making progress. In addition, repeating the words many times helps students build a large sight-word vocabulary.

Students who resist rereading selections need incentives. Besides simply telling the student that rereading is a part of the important practice one does to become a better reader, you might motivate her by having her:

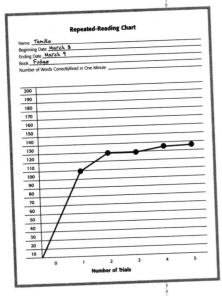

- ◆ read to a friend, family member, or pet,
- ◆ read to a student in a lower grade,
- ◆ read into a tape player to record the session,
- ◆ set a reading-rate goal for a given piece of text and try to exceed that goal in successive readings.

5. Cueing phrase boundaries in text

One of the characteristics of proficient (fluent) readers is the ability to group words together in meaningful units—syntactically appropriate phrases. "Proficient reading is characterized not only by fast and accurate word recognition, but also by readers' word chunking or phrasing behavior while reading connected discourse." (Rasinski, 1989) Students who are having trouble with comprehension may not be putting words together in meaningful phrases or chunks as they read. Their oral reading is characterized by a choppy, word-by-word delivery that impedes comprehension. These students need instruction in phrasing written text into appropriate segments.

One way to help students learn to recognize and use natural English phrase boundaries—and thus improve their phrasing, fluency, and comprehension—is phrase-cued text practice. Phrase-cued text is a short passage marked by a slash (or some other visual) at the end of each phrase break. The longer pause at the end of the sentence is marked by a double slash (//). The teacher models good oral reading, and students practice with the marked text. Later, students apply their skills to the same text, unmarked. Have students practice the skill orally for 10 minutes daily.

Here's an example:

In the summer/I like/to swim/at the beach.//

Although it's very hot/I like the idea/

of being in the cool water

all day.// Summer truly is/

my favorite time/of the year.//

6. Providing students with easy reading materials

Students need an enormous amount of individualized reading practice in decodable materials that are not too difficult (Beck & Juel, 1995; Samuels, Schermer & Reinking, 1992). Aim for at least 30 minutes of independent reading every day. Some should occur in school, and some can occur at home. Fluency develops through a great deal of practice reading texts in which students can use sound-spelling strategies (as opposed to contextual strategies) to figure out a majority of the unfamiliar words. In the early grades, there must be a match between instruction in phonics and reading practice—hence the need for practice stories and poems that are decodable (Blevins, 2002). This match encourages students to adopt sound-spelling strategies and at the same time, through extensive practice reading text after text after text, leads to fluent reading. It is critical that practice reading materials be at a child's independent or instructional reading level, *not* at the child's frustration level. In other words, the student's reading accuracy (the proportion of words read correctly) should be above 90 percent. During individualized practice, students may be reading at different levels. They read aloud "quietly" to themselves as the teacher walks around listening to each child for a minute or so while still monitoring the group as a whole. Students need time to figure out unfamiliar words through phonics patterns. Expecting students to read fluently when they are not fluent only encourages guessing and memorization.

Using Poetry to Build Fluency

Poetry lends itself beautifully to fluency instruction and practice. The length and natural rhythms of most poems give them a musical quality that's enjoyable to listen to and perform. Poetry often contains a wide range of punctuation and phrasing, two key aspects of fluency. In addition, poems are fun ways to practice one's decoding skills.

The poems in this collection are divided into four categories:

1. Poems for Partners and Small Groups

These poems are ideal for students to read together. Some contain multiple parts perfect for Reader's Theater; others have repetitive stanzas that are fun for choral reading. Working together gives students an opportunity to provide peers with constructive feedback, thereby verbalizing their understanding of fluent reading.

2. Poems to Build Intonation and Phrasing

These poems focus on varying the pace and expression of oral readings. The variety of sentence types and phrase boundaries helps students to pay attention to these important aspects of reading. In addition, the chunking of text into meaningful units, line by line, is one way to introduce or reinforce aspects of grammar useful in reading fluently (subject, predicate, prepositional phrases).

3. Poems to Build Recognition of Phonics Patterns and Sight Words

These poems focus on one or two key phonics patterns common to early reading materials. The repetition of the patterns helps students to easily recognize these larger word chunks so useful in decoding longer words.

4. Poems for Repeated Readings

These poems are more complex and comprehensive. They require students to pull together all aspects of fluent reading and encourage students to practice enough so that a formal, dramatic reading is the ultimate result.

Instructional Routine

Use the following routine for introducing each poem.

STEP 1: Distribute copies of the poem or write the poem on chart paper. As an alternative, make a transparency of the poem and show it on the overhead projector.

STEP 2: Read aloud the poem. Highlight one or two aspects of fluency, such as intonation or phrasing. Discuss these aspects of fluency and model them using selected sentences or phrases from the poem.

STEP 3: Do an echo reading of the poem. Read aloud each stanza and have students repeat using the same pace, accuracy, and expression.

STEP 4: Assign the poem to partners, small groups, or individuals based on the goal of each poem. For example, poems designed for repeated readings should be assigned to individuals, whereas poems for choral readings should be assigned to small groups.

STEP 5: Provide time throughout the week for students to practice reading aloud their poems. Circulate and listen in. Provide feedback on key aspects of fluent reading. Then, allow students to share their readings at the end of the week.

Above all, have fun with the poems in this book. Poems are like language amusement parks; they represent the works of those playing with language in rhythmic and creative ways. Sharing the joys of written language with students is a wonderful and valuable gift.

Boom, Boom, Ain't It Great to Be Crazy?

—TRADITIONAL

A horse and a flea and three blind mice
Sat on a curbstone shooting dice.
The horse he slipped and fell on the flea.
"Whoops," said the flea, "there's a horse on me!"

Boom, boom, ain't it great to be crazy?
Boom, boom, ain't it great to be crazy?
Giddy and foolish the whole day through,
Boom, boom, ain't it great to be crazy?

Way down south where the bananas grow,
A flea stepped on an elephant's toe.
The elephant cried, with tears in his eyes,
"Why don't you pick on someone your own size?"

Boom, boom, ain't it great to be crazy?
Boom, boom, ain't it great to be crazy?
Giddy and foolish the whole day through,
Boom, boom, ain't it great to be crazy?

Cloud Brothers

BY RAMSON LOMATEWAMA

All voices:
Four directions
cloud brothers
share one sky.

> *First voice:*
> Each has its own path.
>
> *Second voice:*
> Each has its own mood.
>
> *Third voice:*
> Each has its own face.

First voice:
The cloud brothers are many
but they are one family.

Second voice:
The cloud brothers are scattered
but they are one spirit.

Third voice:
They mingle
within themselves
changing with every moment.

Continued

First and second voices:
They tell us
that we too
are brothers
on this land.

Third voice:
And
like our cloud brothers

All voices:
we are all yellow
⠀⠀⠀⠀as are the sunrise clouds
we are all white
⠀⠀⠀⠀as are the noonday clouds
we are all black
⠀⠀⠀⠀as are the thunder clouds
we are all red
⠀⠀⠀⠀as are the sunset clouds.

Second and third voices:
So let us look up to our cloud brothers
as one family
and one spirit.

First voice:
For we are truly different

All voices:
and yet
⠀⠀⠀⠀we are truly the same.

Limericks

An Old Man With a Beard

BY *EDWARD LEAR*

There was an Old Man with a beard
Who said, "It is just as I feared!—
    Two Owls and a Hen,
    Four Larks and a Wren
Have all built their nests in my beard."

A Young Farmer of Leeds

—*ANONYMOUS*

There was a young farmer of Leeds
Who swallowed six packets of seeds.
    It soon came to pass
    He was covered with grass,
And he couldn't sit down for the weeds.

How Many Legs?

BY MARY SULLIVAN

A starfish has five legs,
A spider has eight.

I have only two legs,
(That's why I'm always late.)

A cow has four legs,
As do a pig and a horse.

Dogs have four legs,
So do cats, of course!

Flies have six legs,
And so do tiny ants.

Centipedes have so many legs,
They'll never learn to dance!

A snail has just one leg,
But always makes do.

A snake has none at all—
Guess I'm lucky to have two!

Mom's Allergic

BY MARY SULLIVAN

I'm not allowed to keep the snake
'Cause Mom's allergic, for goodness sake!

It comes to me as some surprise
That snakes cause sneezing
And watery eyes.

I've told her this snake
Is perfectly harmless.
It's clawless, it's toothless,
It's stingless, it's armless!

And to help make my point
This snake is not charmless:
It's quiet, it's pretty,
It's dry to the touch.
It's gentle, it's friendly,
It doesn't eat much.

Aw, what the heck,
I know it's no use.
(This allergy thing
Is some fancy excuse!)

Languages My Neighbors Speak

BY LINDA BENDOR

The man at the shoe repair
        speaks Spanish
        Buenos Dias.

The lady at the bakery
        speaks French
        Bonjour.

The man at the falafel stand
        speaks Hebrew
        Shalom.

The lady at the fish market
        speaks Japanese
        Konichiwa.

Chinese, Swahili, Russian, Greek—
any language that I seek
are languages my neighbors speak!

Perfect Poems With Strategies for Building Fluency: Grades 5–6   Scholastic Teaching Resources

If You Should Meet a
Crocodile

—TRADITIONAL

If you should meet a crocodile
    Don't take a stick and poke him;
Ignore the welcome in his smile,
    Be careful not to stroke him.

For as he sleeps upon the Nile,
    He thinner gets, and thinner.
And whenever you meet a crocodile,
    He's ready for his dinner.

Do You Carrot All for Me?

—TRADITIONAL

Do you carrot all for me?
My heart beets for you,
With your turnip nose
And your radish face,
You are a peach.
If we cantaloupe,
Lettuce marry:
Weed make a swell pear.

Perfect Poems With Strategies for Building Fluency: Grades 5–6   Scholastic Teaching Resources

Animals, Animals

—TRADITIONAL

I've Got a Dog

I've got a dog as thin as a rail.
He's got fleas all over his tail;
Every time his tail goes flop,
The fleas on the bottom all hop to the top.

The Codfish

The codfish lays ten thousand eggs,
    The homely hen lays one.
The codfish never cackles
    To tell you what she's done.
And so we scorn the codfish,
    While the humble hen we prize,
Which only goes to show you
    That it pays to advertise.

The Centipede

A centipede was happy quite,
    Until a frog in fun
Said, "Pray, which leg comes after which?"
This raised her mind to such a pitch,
She lay distracted in the ditch
    Considering how to run.

The Key of the Kingdom

—TRADITIONAL

This is the key of the kingdom:
In that kingdom is a city,
In that city is a town,
In that town there is a street,
In that street there winds a lane,
In that lane there is a yard,
In that yard there is a house,
In the house there waits a room,
In that room there is a bed,
On that bed there is a basket,
A basket of flowers.

Flowers in the basket,
Basket on the bed,
Bed in the chamber,
Chamber in the house,
House in the weedy yard,
Yard in the winding lane,
Lane in the broad street,
Street in the high town,
Town in the city,
City in the kingdom:
This is the key of the kingdom.

Seven Days of Supper

BY DOROTHY JEAN SKLAR

On Monday, Mom makes spaghetti.
On Tuesday, Dad's dish is rice and beans.
On Wednesday, Sister fixes fish sticks.
Thursday? Time for Grandma's collard greens.
Friday is Uncle's pork chop suey.
Come Saturday, Auntie serves sardines.
I can hardly wait for Sunday.
That's when I decide on the cuisine:
Peanut-butter-potato-chip cake
Filled with fudge-ripple-mint ice cream!
A strange choice, you say, for supper?
This meal's better balanced than it seems.
And after a week with no dessert,
This is the dinner of my dreams!

Earth, What Will You Give Me?

BY BEVERLY MCLOUGHLAND

Earth, what will you give me
In summer,
In summer,
Earth, what will you give me
In summer
Serene?

I'll give you my fields
Made of lilies,
Of lilies,
I'll give you my fields
Made of lilies
And green.

And what will you give me
In autumn,
In autumn,
And what will you give me
In autumn
So bold?

I'll give you my leaves
Made of maple,
Of maple,
I'll give you my leaves
Made of maple
And gold.

And what will you give me
In winter,
In winter,
And what will you give me
In winter
So light?

I'll give you my stars
Made of crystal,
Of crystal,
I'll give you my stars
Made of crystal
And white.

And what will you give me
In springtime,
In springtime,
And what will you give me
In springtime
So new?

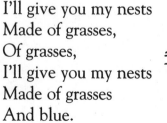

I'll give you my nests
Made of grasses,
Of grasses,
I'll give you my nests
Made of grasses
And blue.

Perfect Poems With Strategies for Building Fluency: Grades 5–6 Scholastic Teaching Resources

To Be Answered in Our Next Issue

—TRADITIONAL

When a great tree falls
And people aren't near,
Does it make a noise
If no one can hear?
And which came first,
The hen or the egg?
This impractical question
We ask and then beg.
Some wise men say
It's beyond their ken.
Did anyone ever
Ask the hen?

Wondering

Ezra Smathers: Oregon Territory, August, 1843

BY BOBBI KATZ

All I asked was, "Pa, you reckon
    that we're halfway there?"
Pa snarled back like a wild she-bear,
"You ask that question ten times a day!"
(I don't. No, I don't. But I didn't dare say.)

When we left Independence four months ago,
I didn't know time could ever run so slow.
At first it was fun riding up here all day,
seeing new places along the way—
    deserts and prairies—
           a wild river flood
with our wheels cutting ruts through the dust and the mud—
seeing strange critters I've never seen before—
    moose and rattlers—
        buffalo by the score.

Continued

Perfect Poems With Strategies for Building Fluency: Grades 5–6 Scholastic Teaching Resources

Past Laramie,
South Pass,
then Fort Hall—
through woods so full of giant trees
no sky poked through at all.

When we stop for the night, it's
        "Fetch water."
                    "Find wood."
        "Rock the baby."
                    "Stir the pot."
        "Listen up."
                    "Be good."

And always, always, always, it's
"Don't stray away!"
And never, never, never is it
"Run off and play!"
Ma says in Vancouver,
there'll be playing time to spare.
I just wonder what Pa reckons.
Are we halfway there?

Zoons

BY FLORENCE E. SULLIVAN

Zinkety-zankety zoons,
It's fun to find words
That rhyme with *zoons*—
Cartoons, buffoons,
Balloons, and *tunes.*
Some animal words
Rhyme with *zoons*—
Raccoons and *loons,*
Cocoons, baboons.
Yes, many words
Rhyme with *zoons*—
You can use *prunes,*
Or *moons,* or *spoons.*
And then you're not done;
You've just begun
Finding words
To rhyme with *zoons*—
Zinkety-zankety,
Zinkety-zankety,
Zinkety-zankety zoons.

Perfect Poems With Strategies for Building Fluency: Grades 5–6   Scholastic Teaching Resources

Foul Shot

BY EDWIN A. HOEY

With two 60s stuck on the scoreboard
And two seconds hanging on the clock,
The solemn boy in the center of eyes,
Squeezed by silence,
Seeks out the line with his feet,
Soothes his hands along his uniform,
Gently drums the ball against the floor,
Then measures the waiting net,
Raises the ball on his right hand,
Balances it with his left,
Calms it with fingertips,
Breathes,
Crouches,
Waits,
And then through a stretching of stillness,
Nudges it upward.

The ball
Slides up and out.
Lands,
Leans,
Wobbles,
Wavers,
Hesitates,
Exasperates,
Plays it coy
Until every face begs with unsounding screams—
And then,
       And then,
              And then,
Right before ROAR-UP,
Dives down and through.

Leap Year Lament

BY JACQUELINE SWEENEY

Leaping spiders
Leaping goats
"Leaping Lizards!"
    Too.
I'll play Leagfrog
'til I croak, but Leaping
birthdays will not
    Do!
My friend, Alicia's
eight years old while
I'm just turning
    TWO.

Pass the ice cream
Pass the hats
Pass the presents
    Please!
When Alicia's
twelve years old,
I'll be turning
    THREE.

Light those candles
Cut that cake
Sing to me once
    More!
For when Alicia's
"sweet sixteen"
I'll just be turning
    FOUR
        !

Perfect Poems With Strategies for Building Fluency: Grades 5–6   Scholastic Teaching Resources

The Joke You Just Told

—TRADITIONAL

The joke you just told isn't funny one bit.
It's pointless and dull, wholly lacking in wit.
It's so old and stale, it's beginning to smell!
Besides, it's the one I was going to tell.

Whether the Weather

—ANONYMOUS

Whether the weather be fine
Or whether the weather be not
Whether the weather be cold
Or whether the weather be hot—
We'll weather the weather
Whatever the weather
Whether we like it or not!

The Goops

BY GELETT BURGESS

The Goops they lick their fingers,
And the Goops they lick their knives;
They spill their broth on the tablecloth—
Oh, they lead disgusting lives!
The Goops they talk while eating,
And loud and fast they chew;
And that is why I am glad that I
Am not a Goop—are you?

The Goops are gluttonous and rude,
They gug and gumble with their food;
They throw their crumbs upon the floor,
And at dessert they tease for more;
They will not eat their soup and bread
But like to gobble sweets, instead,
And this is why I oft decline,
When I am asked to stay and dine!

Time *for* Bed

BY AMANDA MILLER

"I'm not a child!" I told my mom
When she said to go to bed.
"I can stay up just as late as you,
I don't need to rest my head."

Mom smiled at me and then she said,
"Well, climb back on the couch.
Try to keep your eyes wide open
And make sure that you don't slouch."

I did O.K. the first half-hour,
I didn't blink an eye.
Though it was hard to hide my sleepiness,
I really sure did try!

But in the final minutes
Of my very favorite show,
Mom said I started snoring,
But I was asleep . . . so I don't know!

Perfect Poems With Strategies for Building Fluency: Grades 5–6   Scholastic Teaching Resources

See How They Run!

BY GRACE MAYR

Run is a word with meanings galore.
I'll think of some. You think of more.
Run is a break in your mother's hose;
Run is what paint does all over your clothes.
You run for the bus and for office, too;
Prices run high, but that's nothing new.
You run up a seam, run before you jump,
Run onto a bargain, and over a bump.

Peaches run fine and big this season;
Sailboats run with the wind with reason.
A run in baseball can win the game;
A horse run too hard will often go lame.
And on we could run for many a day
Compounding nouns—rundown, runaway,
Runoff, run-in, run-out, runabout.
Please! Please! No need to shout,
For I've run down! But it's been fun
Naming ways to use the word *run*.

Spelling Test

BY LINDA B. ROSS

I had a spelling test today.
I hope that I did well,
But some of the words on my spelling test
Were very hard to spell!

I'll give you some examples
To show you what I mean:
Spaghetti, spare, and *sparkle,*
Skeleton, and *machine!*

Here are more examples;
These words are difficult, too:
Skiing and *skyscraper,*
Statue, stitch, and *stew!*

Am I a very good speller?
Today I'm not too sure.
I'll let you know tomorrow
When I get my spelling score.

Perfect Poems With Strategies for Building Fluency: Grades 5–6   Scholastic Teaching Resources

The Red Ball

BY LIZA CHARLESWORTH

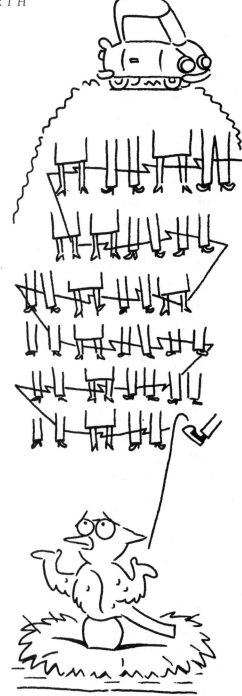

The red ball
slipped from
the baby's hands,
bounced,
bounced,
bounced,
down the cement stairs,
zoomed past
the fire hydrant,
raced through
a championship game
of hopscotch,
crossed the street,
rolled under
a blue car,
then zigzagged between
two dozen pairs
of feet,
until one sneaker
kicked it up
into the air
with such force
it landed
with a PLUNK!
in the tidy nest
of a jay—
who, by the way,
is still waiting
for the curious thing
to hatch.

City I Love

BY LEE BENNETT HOPKINS

In the city
I live in—
city I love—
mornings wake
to
swishes, swashes,
sputters
of sweepers
swooshing litter
from gutters.

In the city
I live in—
city I love—
afternoons pulse
with
people hurrying,
scurrying—
races of faces
pacing to
must-get-there
places.

In the city
I live in—
city I love—
nights shimmer
with lights
competing
with stars
above
unknown heights.

In the city
I live in—
city I love—
as dreams
start to creep
my city
of senses
lulls
me
to sleep.

Perfect Poems With Strategies for Building Fluency: Grades 5–6   Scholastic Teaching Resources

Some Poems

BY BEVERLY McLOUGHLAND

Some poems
Want to get written
So badly—
They don't care
If you are
Sound asleep
At 3 o'clock
In the morning. No.
They just
Barge in,
Shake you
Awake,
Drag you
Out of bed,
Plop you
In a chair,
Stick a pencil
In your hand—
And *make* you
Write.

A Thunderstorm

—TRADITIONAL

Boom, bang, boom, bang,
Rumpety, lumpety, bump!
Zoom, zam, zoom, zam,
Clippity, clappity, clump!
Rustles and bustles,
And swishes and zings!
What wonderful sounds
A thunderstorm brings.

Michael Finnegan

—Traditional

There was an old man named Michael Finnegan.
He had whiskers on his chinnegan.
They fell out and then grew in again.
Poor old Michael Finnegan,
Begin again.

There was an old man named Michael Finnegan.
He went fishing with a pin again.
Caught a fish and dropped it in again.
Poor old Michael Finnegan,
Begin again.

There was an old man named Michael Finnegan.
He grew fat and then grew thin again.
Then he died and had to begin again.
Poor old Michael Finnegan,
Begin again.

BEFORE   AFTER

Have You Ever Seen?

—TRADITIONAL

Have you ever seen a sheet on a river bed?
Or a single hair from a hammer's head?
Has the foot of a mountain any toes?
And is there a pair of garden hose?

Does the needle ever wink its eye?
Why doesn't the wing of a building fly?
Can you tickle the ribs of a parasol?
Or open the trunk of a tree at all?

Are the teeth of a rake ever going to bite?
Have the hands of a clock any left or right?
Can the garden plot be deep and dark?
And what is the sound of the birch's bark?

Perfect Poems With Strategies for Building Fluency: Grades 5–6   Scholastic Teaching Resources

Funny Foods

—ANONYMOUS

A Peanut Sat on a Railroad Track

A peanut sat on a railroad track,
Its heart was all a-flutter;
The five-fifteen came rushing by —
Toot! Toot! Peanut butter!

One Summer at Tea

There was a young lady named Perkins
Who had a great fondness for gherkins;
    One summer at tea
    She ate twenty-three
Which pickled her internal workin's.

A Man of Bengal

There once was a man of Bengal
Who was asked to a fancy dress ball;
    He murmured: "I'll risk it
    And go as a biscuit . . ."
But a dog ate him up in the hall.

Words

BY GLENDA GREVE

I like stand-up words.
   straight   still
I like sit-down words.
   slide   spill
I like scary words.
   Whooo's there?
I like noisy words.
   Bang!   Blare!
I like happy words.
   grin   giggle
I like funny words.
   hoot   wiggle
I like sleepy words.
   soft pillow
I like sad words.
   weeping willow
I like pretty words.
   tinkle   silk
I like eating words.
   bread   milk

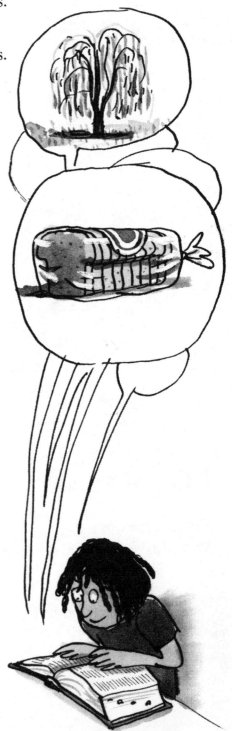

Perfect Poems With Strategies for Building Fluency: Grades 5–6   Scholastic Teaching Resources

A Magic Chant

BY BOBBI KATZ

Mumbo
    jumbo
        griggle
            grumbo!
Fista
    fasta
        lasta
            pasta!
Joga
    voga
        foga
            VOO!
Ickle
    pickle
        parsley stew!

Say these words by day or night.
Get them absolutely right.
Learn them and you'll be prepared
For anything that makes you scared.

Mumbo
    jumbo
        griggle
            grumbo!
Fista
    fasta
        lasta
            pasta!
Joga
    voga
        foga
            VOO!
Ickle
    pickle
        parsley stew!

Animal Groups

BY MEISH GOLDISH

Some animals
Live in a group.
A special name
Describes each troop:
A herd of cattle,
A gaggle of geese,
A flock of sheep
With woolly fleece.
A pride of lions,
A bevy of quails,
A litter of puppies
With wagging tails.
A school of fish,
A swarm of flies,
A pack of wolves
With watchful eyes.
A brood of hens,
A nest of birds,
Animal groups
With special words!

Perfect Poems With Strategies for Building Fluency: Grades 5–6   Scholastic Teaching Resources

A Secret in My Pocket

BY KAREN BAICKER

I have a secret in my pocket.
It goes everywhere with me.
My secret is invisible,
Impossible to see.

It's the twinkle in the stars,
And the sprinkle-covered cone.
It's everything that makes me laugh
Aloud when I'm alone.

It's the maple in my syrup,
And the bubble in my bath,
The streamers on my bicycle,
My hidden garden path.

It's the whiskers on a kitten,
And the bumble in a bee.
It's every little secret thing
I've wanted it to be.

Color Song

—TRADITIONAL

Red is the color for an apple to eat.
Red is the color for cherries, too.
Red is the color for strawberries.
I like red, don't you?

Blue is the color for the big blue sky.
Blue is the color for baby things, too.
Blue is the color of my sister's eyes.
I like blue, don't you?

Yellow is the color for the great big sun.
Yellow is the color for lemonade, too.
Yellow is the color of a baby chick.
I like yellow, don't you?

Green is the color for the leaves on the trees.
Green is the color for green peas, too.
Green is the color of a watermelon.
I like green, don't you?

Orange is the color for oranges.
Orange is the color for carrots, too.
Orange is the color of a jack-o'-lantern.
I like orange, don't you?

Purple is the color for a bunch of grapes.
Purple is the color for grape juice, too.
Purple is the color for a violet.
I like purple, don't you?

Perfect Poems With Strategies for Building Fluency: Grades 5–6   Scholastic Teaching Resources

Mary Had a Little Lamb

—ANONYMOUS

Mary had a little lamb,
A lobster and some prunes,
A glass of milk, a piece of pie,
And then some macaroons.

It made the busy waiters grin
To see her order so,
And when they carried Mary out,
Her face was white as snow.

Old Hogan's Goat

—TRADITIONAL

Old Hogan's goat was feeling fine,
Ate six red shirts from off the line;
Old Hogan grabbed him by the back
And tied him to the railroad track.
Now when the train came into sight,
That goat grew pale and green with fright;
He heaved a sigh, as if in pain,
Coughed up those shirts and flagged the train!

Paul Bunyan

BY MEISH GOLDISH

Oh, he came from Minnesota,
So a lot of people say.
He could chop a hundred trees down
In less than half a day!

He was famous as a lumberjack,
His muscles were like rocks!
He hauled a heavy load of logs
With Babe, his big blue ox!

Tall Paul Bunyan,
Chopping down those trees!
In the forest with his giant axe,
He cleared the way with ease!

Oh, Paul was quite a logger,
Full of energy and pep!
He could walk across a river
In just one giant step!

Oh, Paul could lift a mountain
Just as easy as a wink!
They say he dug the Great Lakes
Just so Babe could have a drink!

Tall Paul Bunyan,
Chopping down those trees!
In the forest with his giant axe,
He cleared the way with ease!

Night-Lights

—ANONYMOUS

There is no need to light a
    night-light
On a light night like tonight;
For a night-light's light's a
    slight light
When the moonlight's white
    and bright.

Perfect Poems With Strategies for Building Fluency: Grades 5–6   Scholastic Teaching Resources

He Had a Dream

BY MEISH GOLDISH

Perfect Poems With Strategies for Building Fluency: Grades 5–6   Scholastic Teaching Resources

"I have a dream!"
"I have a dream!"
These were the words
Of Martin Luther King.
What was his dream?
What was his dream?
Tell us the dream
Of Martin Luther King.

Dr. King wished,
Dr. King prayed
That one day all people
Would live unafraid.
Dr. King cared
For blacks and for whites.
He wanted all people
To share equal rights.

Continued

"I have a dream!"
"I have a dream!"
These were the words
Of Martin Luther King.
What was his dream?
What was his dream?
Tell us the dream
Of Martin Luther King.

Dr. King marched,
Dr. King spoke
Of a world full of justice
For all kinds of folk.
Dr. King cared
For me and for you.
By working together,
His dream can come true!

"I have a dream!"
"I have a dream!"
These were the words
Of Martin Luther King.
What was his dream?
What was his dream?
Tell us the dream
Of Martin Luther King.

American Heritage

BY ELSIE WALUSH

The Declaration of Independence,
The Constitution with its Bill of Rights:
These are the bulwarks of our heritage,
These are our nation's guiding lights.

Freedom of speech, freedom of press,
Freedom to worship as we please,
The right to assemble, the right to petition,
Are some of the freedoms we recite with ease.

The right to life, the right to liberty,
The right to pursuit of happiness,
The right to equality, the right to security,
The right to live without undue stress.

But what of the many other rights,
Not written in our laws—
The right to labor, the right to suffer,
The right to fight for freedom's cause?

For these are rights our forefathers chose,
When they laid our country's foundation,
And these are the rights we must assume
To preserve our precious nation.

Revolutionary Tea

—TRADITIONAL

There was an old lady lived over the sea,
And she was an Island Queen;
Her daughter lived off in a new countrie,
With an ocean of water between.
The old lady's pockets were full of gold,
But never contented was she,
So she called on her daughter to pay her a tax
Of threepence a pound on her tea,
Of threepence a pound on her tea.

"Now Mother, dear Mother," the daughter replied,
"I shan't do the thing you ax;
I'm willing to pay a fair price for the tea,
But never the three-penny tax."
"You shall," quoth the mother, and reddened with rage,
"For you're my own daughter, you see.
And sure 'tis quite proper the daughter should pay
Her mother a tax on her tea,
Her mother a tax on her tea."

The tea was conveyed to the daughter's door,
All down by the ocean's side.
And the bouncing girl poured out every pound,
In the dark and boiling tide.
And then she called out to the Island Queen,
"Oh Mother, dear Mother," quoth she,
"Your tea may you have when 'tis steeped enough,
But never a tax from me,
But never a tax from me."

In this old song, written about the Boston Tea Party, the "Island Queen" is Britain, and the "daughter" is the American colonies.

Perfect Poems With Strategies for Building Fluency: Grades 5–6   Scholastic Teaching Resources

I Don't Want To

BY JACK PRELUTSKY

I don't want to play on the sidewalk.
I don't want to sit on the stoop.
I don't want to lick any ice cream.
I don't want to slurp any soup.
I don't want to listen to music.
I don't want to look at cartoons.
I don't want to read any stories.
I don't want to blow up balloons.

I don't want to dig in the garden.
I don't want to roll on the rug.
I don't want to wrestle the puppy.
I don't want to give you a hug.
I don't want to shoot any baskets.
I don't want to bang on my drum.
I don't want to line up my soldiers.
I don't want to whistle or hum.

I don't want to program my robot.
I don't want to strum my guitar.
I don't want to use my computer.
I don't want to wind up my car.
I don't want to color with crayons.
I don't want to model with clay.
I don't want to stop my not wanting . . .
I'm having that kind of day.

Perfect Poems With Strategies for Building Fluency: Grades 5–6   Scholastic Teaching Resources

Granny and the Broomstick

BY ANDREW MATTHEWS

Granny found the broom
When she was clearing out the shed.
"Just the job for sweeping up the garden!"
Granny said.

That night, as Granny lay in bed
With curlers in her hair,
She heard a crafty, creepy sound
Come swishing up the stairs.

The door swung wide, and something tall
Came jumping in the room.
"Good gracious me!" cried Granny.
"It's a jumping, walking broom!"

When Granny touched the broom, they both
Went floating to the ceiling.
"It tickles!" chuckled Granny.
"What a most peculiar feeling!"

They flew out of the bedroom
With a roaring, soaring ZOOM!
"It's just as well you left that window open,"
Said the broom.

Continued

They flew as low as dustbin lids
And gave two cats a fright.
They flew as high as mountains
Up into the starry night.

"Fancy a trip to Timbuktu?"
The broom asked. "Paris? Rome?"
"I'm feeling rather tired just now," said Granny.
"Take me home."

The broom flew silently above
The dark and sleepy streets
And slipped the gently-snoring Granny
Back between her sheets.

When Granny woke next morning
And remembered all she'd seen,
She rubbed her eyes and said, "I've had
A funny sort of dream!

Imagine someone my age
On a broomstick—what a sight!"
But from then onwards, Granny dreamed
Of flying every night.

Mr. Nobody

—ANONYMOUS

I know a funny little man,
        As quiet as a mouse,
Who does the mischief that is done
        In everybody's house!
There's no one ever sees his face,
        And yet we all agree
That every plate we break was cracked
        By Mr. Nobody.

'Tis he who always tears our books,
        Who leaves the door ajar,
He pulls the buttons from our shirts,
        And scatters pins afar;
That squeaking door will always squeak,
        For, prithee, don't you see,
We leave the oiling to be done
        By Mr. Nobody.

The finger marks upon the door
        By none of us are made;
We never leave the blinds unclosed,
        To let the curtains fade.
The ink we never spill; the boots
        That lying round you see
Are not our boots—they all belong
        To Mr. Nobody.

My Brother Bert

BY TED HUGHES

Pets are the hobby of my brother Bert.
He used to go to school with a mouse in his shirt.

His hobby it grew, as some hobbies will,
And grew and GREW and GREW until—

Oh don't breathe a word, pretend you haven't heard.
A simply appalling thing has occurred—

The very thought makes me iller and iller:
Bert's brought home a gigantic gorilla!

If you think that's really not such a scare,
What if it quarrels with his grizzly bear?

You still think you could keep your head?
What if the lion from under the bed

And the four ostriches that deposit
Their football eggs in his bedroom closet

And the aardvark out of his bottom drawer
All danced out and joined in the roar?

Continued

Perfect Poems With Strategies for Building Fluency: Grades 5–6   Scholastic Teaching Resources

What if the pangolins were to caper
Out of their nests behind the wallpaper?

With the fifty sorts of bats
That hang on his hatstand like old hats,

And out of a shoebox the excitable platypus
Along with the ocelot or jungle-cattypus?

The wombat, the dingo, the gecko, the grampus—
How they would shake the house with their rumpus!

Not to forget the bandicoot
Who would certainly peer from his battered old boot.

Why it could be a dreadful day,
And what, oh what, would the neighbors say!

The Song of the Camel

BY CHARLES EDWARD CARRYL

Canary-birds feed on sugar and seed,
Parrots have crackers to crunch;
And, as for the poodles, they tell me the noodles
Have chickens and cream for their lunch.
But there's never a question
About MY digestion—
ANYTHING does for me!

Cats, you're aware, can repose in a chair,
Chickens can roost upon rails;
Puppies are able to sleep in a stable,
And oysters can slumber in pails.
But no one supposes
A poor Camel dozes—
ANY PLACE does for me!

Continued

Lambs are enclosed where it's never exposed,
Coops are constructed for hens;
Kittens are treated to houses well heated,
And pigs are protected by pens.
But a Camel comes handy
Wherever it's sandy—
ANYWHERE does for me!

People would laugh if you rode a giraffe,
Or mounted the back of an ox;
It's nobody's habit to ride on a rabbit,
Or try to bestraddle a fox.
But as for a Camel, he's
Ridden by families—
ANY LOAD does for me!

A snake is as round as a hole in the ground,
And weasels are wavy and sleek;
And no alligator could every be straighter
Than lizards that live in a creek.
But a Camel's all lumpy
And bumpy and humpy—
ANY SHAPE does for me!

From The Cares of a Caretaker

BY WALLACE IRWIN

A nice old lady by the sea
Was neat as she was plain,
And every time the tide came in
She swept it back again.

And when the sea untidy grew
And waves began to beat,
She took her little garden rake
And raked it smooth and neat.

And when the gulls came strolling by,
She drove them shrilly back,
Remarking that it spoiled the beach,
"The way them birds do track."

Continued

She stopped the little sea urchins
That traveled by in pairs,
And washed their dirty faces clean
And combed their little hairs.

She spread white napkins on the surf
With which she fumed and fussed.
"When it ain't covered up," she said,
"It gits all over dust."

She didn't like to see the ships
With all the waves act free,
And so she got a painted sign
Which read: "Keep off the Sea."

But dust and splutter as she might,
Her work was sadly vain;
However oft she swept the beach,
The tides came in again.

And she was sometimes wan and worn
When she retired to bed—
"A woman's work ain't never done,"
That nice old lady said.

From
Adventures of
Isabel

BY OGDEN NASH

Isabel met an enormous bear;
Isabel, Isabel didn't care.
The bear was hungry, the bear was ravenous,
The bear's big mouth was cruel and cavernous.
The bear said, Isabel, glad to meet you,
How do, Isabel, now I'll eat you!
Isabel, Isabel, didn't worry,
Isabel didn't scream or scurry.
She washed her hands and she straightened her hair up.
Then Isabel quietly ate the bear up.

Continued

Once on a night as black as pitch
Isabel met a wicked old witch.
The witch's face was cross and wrinkled,
The witch's gums with teeth were sprinkled.
Ho, ho, Isabel! the old witch crowed,
I'll turn you into an ugly toad!
Isabel, Isabel, didn't worry,
Isabel didn't scream or scurry.
She showed no rage and she showed no rancor,
But she turned the witch into milk and drank her.

Isabel met a hideous giant,
Isabel continued self-reliant.
The giant was hairy, the giant was horrid,
He had one eye in the middle of his forehead.
Good morning, Isabel, the giant said.
I'll grind your bones to make my bread.
Isabel, Isabel, didn't worry.
Isabel didn't scream or scurry.
She nibbled the zwieback that she always fed off,
And when it was gone, she cut the giant's head off.

Perfect Poems With Strategies for Building Fluency: Grades 5–6   Scholastic Teaching Resources

Sick

BY *SHEL SILVERSTEIN*

"I cannot go to school today,"
Said little Peggy Ann McKay.
"I have the measles and the mumps,
A gash, a rash, and purple bumps.
My mouth is wet, my throat is dry,
I'm going blind in my right eye.
My tonsils are as big as rocks,
I've counted sixteen chicken pox
And there's one more—that's seventeen,
And don't you think my face looks green?
My leg is cut, my eyes are blue—
It might be instamatic flu.
I cough and sneeze and gasp and choke,
I'm sure that my left leg is broke—
My hip hurts when I move my chin,
My belly button's caving in,
My back is wrenched, my ankle's sprained,
My 'pendix pains each time it rains.
My nose is cold, my toes are numb,
I have a sliver in my thumb.
My neck is stiff, my voice is weak,
I hardly whisper when I speak.
My tongue is filling up my mouth,
I think my hair is falling out.
My elbow's bent, my spine ain't straight,
My temperature is one-o-eight.
My brain is shrunk, I cannot hear,
There is a hole inside my ear.
I have a hangnail, and my heart is—what?
What's that? What's that you say?
You say today is . . . Saturday?
G'bye, I'm going out to play!"

Fudge

BY JACK PRELUTSKY

Oh, it poured and it rained
and it rained and it poured,
I moped round the house
feeling lonely and bored,
till Father came over
and gave me a nudge,
and said with a smile,
"Let's make chocolate fudge."

Then he gave me a bowl
that we filled to the brim,
it was fun making fudge
in the kitchen with him.
I stirred and I stirred,
but I wasn't too neat,
I got fudge on my hands,
I got fudge on my feet,
I got fudge on my shirt,
I got fudge in my hair,
I got fudge on the table
and fudge on the chair,
I got fudge in my nose,
I got fudge in my ears,
I was covered all over
with chocolate smears.

When the cooking was done,
Father wiped off my face,
and he frowned as he said,
"What a mess in this place!"
He was not really mad
and did not hold a grudge,
and we both ate a mountain
of chocolate fudge.

Perfect Poems With Strategies for Building Fluency: Grades 5–6 Scholastic Teaching Resources